NEW DIRECTIONS IN
MANAGEMENT DEVELOPMENT

Other titles from IES:

Executive Coaching: Inspiring Performance at Work
Carter A
IES Report 379, 2001. ISBN 1 85184 308 6

The Problem of Minority Performance in Organisations
Tackey ND, Tamkin P, Sheppard E
IES Report 375, 2001. ISBN 1 85184 304 3

Succession Planning Demystified
Hirsh W
IES Report 372, 2000. ISBN 1 85184 302 7

Free, Fair and Efficient? Open internal job advertising
Hirsh W, Pollard E, Tamkin P
IES Report 371, 2000. ISBN 1 85184 301 9

Performance Review: Balancing Objectives and Content
Strebler M T, Bevan S, Robinson D
IES Report 370, 2001. ISBN 1 85184 300 0

Employee Returns: Linking HR Performance Indicators to Business Strategy
Carter A, Robinson D
IES Report 365, 2000. ISBN 1 85184 295 0

Learning from Cross-functional Teamwork
Kettley P, Hirsh W
IES Report 356, 2000. ISBN 1 85184 285 3

From People to Profits: The HR link in the service-profit chain
Barber L, Hayday S, Bevan S
IES Report 355, 1999. ISBN 1 85184 284 5

Learning to Manage
Tamkin P, Barber L
IES Report 345, 1998. ISBN 1 85184 273 X

A catalogue of these and over 100 other titles is available from IES,
or on the IES Website, www.employment-studies.co.uk

the | **Institute**
for | **Employment**
       | **Studies**

New Directions in Management Development

W Hirsh
A Carter

IES Research Networks

i|E|S

Report 387

Published by:

THE INSTITUTE FOR EMPLOYMENT STUDIES
Mantell Building
Falmer
Brighton BN1 9RF
UK

Tel.   + 44 (0) 1273 686751
Fax   + 44 (0) 1273 690430

http://www.employment-studies.co.uk

British Cataloguing-in-Publication Data

A catalogue record for this publication is available from the British Library

ISBN 1 85184 316 7

Printed and bound by Antony Rowe Ltd, Eastbourne

The Institute for Employment Studies

IES is an independent, international and apolitical centre of research and consultancy in human resource issues. It works closely with employers in the manufacturing, service and public sectors, government departments, agencies, professional and employee bodies, and foundations. For over 30 years the Institute has been a focus of knowledge and practical experience in employment and training policy, the operation of labour markets and human resource planning and development. IES is a not-for-profit organisation, which has a multidisciplinary staff of over 50. IES expertise is available to all organisations through research, consultancy, publications, and the Internet.

IES aims to help bring about sustainable improvements in employment policy and human resource management. IES achieves this by increasing the understanding and improving the practice of key decision-makers in policy bodies and employing organisations.

The IES Research Networks

This report is the product of a study supported by the IES Research Networks, through which Members finance, and often participate in, applied research on employment issues. Full information on Membership is available from IES on request, or at www.employment-studies.co.uk/networks/.

Acknowledgements

The authors wish to thank those from the organisations listed below who attended IES forum events on the subject of Management Development. The issues raised in their debates stimulated this report:

Anglian Water	Home Office
Arkady Craigmillar	Legal and General
AstraZeneca Group	London Borough of Lewisham
Bank of Scotland	Marks and Spencer
BBC	Naval Manning Agency
British Airways	NHS Leadership Programme
Cabinet Office	Northern Foods
Consignia and Royal Mail	Ordnance Survey
Department of Trade and Industry	Royal Bank of Scotland
East Sussex County Council	Sainsbury's Supermarkets
Foreign and Commonwealth Office	Scottish Equitable
GlaxoSmithKline	Scottish Executive
Halifax	Standard Life Assurance
HM Customs and Excise	Unilever Research

Thanks are also due to Penny Tamkin and Gwen Leeming at IES for help with both the forum events and the production of this report. Penny also provided invaluable comments and suggestions on the report itself.

Contents

Executive Summary

This report on 'New Directions in Management Development' aims to provide an overview of some of the practical challenges facing management development in major UK employing organisations. It is based largely on published research, plus discussions with management development managers who attended two forums held by IES in 2001. These participants represented about thirty large organisations in both private and public sectors, including international companies.

The report covers:

- the changing context in which management development takes place, and some of the resulting challenges for management development practitioners

- some of the trends and 'new directions' in management development practice and some of the practical issues they raise

- the key issues raised by the forum participants in relation to shaping the management development strategies and practices of their own organisations

- where the field of management development may be heading in future, and some things practitioners need to address.

Changes and challenges

Management development faces changing demands made on it. These arise from changes in the nature of organisations, especially the pressure on managers to deal with more or less continuous upheavals in their organisations. There has also been quite a deep shift in ideas about what 'management' is about, much of it captured in the ideas of 'transformational leadership'.

In practical terms, this means placing more emphasis on the skills to:

- create a sense of vision in a fast changing environment
- motivate teams of people and lead them through change
- innovate in products and services and ways of working

At the same time, ideas have also been changing about how best to help managers learn. Fashion has moved away from long formal courses towards training which is nearer to the job, more tailored to individual needs, and more continuous.

Delivering training to meet both changing business needs and changing ideas about development raises some pressing questions for management development practitioners in major organisations. Questions include:

- How should organisations set and communicate their priorities for management development?
- In large and complex organisations, should management development be centralised or devolved?
- Can organisational management development meet the needs of the individual as well as the organisation?
- How can management development deal with an increasingly diverse management population, only some of whom stay in the organisation for a long time?
- How can development be fitted into the busy and stressful lives of managers?
- How can organisations maintain management development during their frequent experiences of organisational upheaval?
- How should the methods of delivering management development take on board theories about how people learn, and the availability of ICT?
- Who should deliver management development, and what roles do HR or training professionals, line managers and employees need to play?
- How do we know whether management development activities are effective?

Trends in delivery

There has been a growth in management development activity, and also change in how it is delivered. The report summarises published evidence on the trends in three broad forms of management development activity: formal training and management education, informal and more personal development, and career development.

Management training still needs to provide a coherent view of what managers need to learn, but delivery needs to be more flexible and to fit into the busy working lives of managers. Formal management training has therefore become more modular, a trend likely to be accelerated by e-learning provision. Its delivery is often outsourced. More managers are also taking higher education qualifications in business and management, either before they enter employment or later through certificates, diplomas or part-time MBAs.

The development of inter-personal and leadership skills is a high priority and not easily achieved through conventional formal training. This demand has led to an explosion of interest in more personal forms of learning support, including mentoring, coaching, 360 degree feedback, project working, learning sets and team facilitation. These forms of learning appear popular with managers themselves, although they are labour intensive to support and difficult to evaluate.

A shift from managed career moves to more open internal job markets, has changed the way in which managers learn from career experience. Most managers receive little support in managing their own career development.

Some management development programmes combine all these three elements of development activity: formal training, personal support and planned work experience. Such high attention is usually reserved for senior managers and 'high potential' staff. These programmes are labour intensive and not easy to extend to the majority of the management workforce.

For the majority of managers, the greater onus on the individual to take responsibility for their own development is increasing the need for better information and advice for managers, so they take good decisions about their own skill and career development.

Line managers have been given a number of important roles in the development of their subordinates, but they may not yet be equipped to carry these out, or really be encouraged to develop others.

Looking to the future

In looking at the future, the diversity of management development provision seems likely to stay with us, as captured in the term 'blended methods' and sourced in a variety of ways as shown in the figure below.

Formal training faces a tension between an increasingly modular approach in which training will be accessed in 'bit sized' pieces as and when required, and a more holistic approach to ensuring that all managers have access to core skills and knowledge at various key career stages.

Meanwhile, more managers will also be accessing formal education and training outside work, through universities and professional bodies.

Personal learning support faces the challenge of resourcing. In practice, formal mentoring and coaching tend to be offered only to senior or high potential managers.

Management development — a more integrated approach

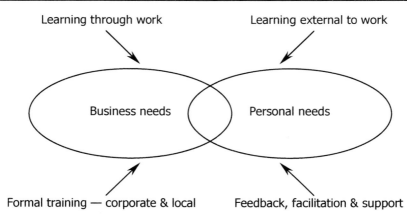

Learning through work

Learning external to work

Business needs

Personal needs

Formal training — corporate & local

Feedback, facilitation & support

Source: IES

On-the-job coaching by many more managers is the most obvious answer to this tension, although it is easier to talk about than to deliver in busy workplaces.

IES suggests a number of priorities for management development over the next few years. These include:

- combining a strong corporate architecture for management development with a capability for 'just in time', and local delivery to meet specific business needs. This requires better high level dialogue about the relationship between business development and management development, both short term and longer term.

- providing better information and advice for individual managers on how to think about their future direction in career terms and their learning needs.

- mainstreaming the skills to manage your own development and to support the development of others within core management training. These skills include those of 'manager as coach' but also go wider and include informal career mentoring.

- finding ways of delivering more stretching and stimulating management development to the whole population of managers, not just those in very senior posts or identified as 'high potential'.

- evaluation and knowledge transfer remain areas of unease. The challenge here is more practical than theoretical: what can organisations do in a sustained way to evaluate management development activities, and to help managers share their learning more effectively?

1. Introduction

This report aims to provide an overview of some of the practical challenges of management development in major UK employing organisations. It is based largely on discussions with management development managers who attended two forums held by IES in 2001. These participants represented about thirty large organisations in both private and public sectors, including international companies. We do not claim that this was in any way a representative sample, even of large organisations. However, they shared many common concerns and saw a number of the same trends in their approaches to management development. Their debate was so lively that we felt it was worth committing some of it to paper. The phrase 'forum participants' will be used when referring to this group in the text of this report.

We also draw on published material and a number of relevant IES research projects on topics including: the skills needed by managers (Kettley and Strebler, 1997), the use of competencies (Strebler and Bevan, 1996), 360 degree feedback (Kettley, 1997), management learning (Tamkin and Barber, 1998), cross-functional teamwork (Kettley and Hirsh, 2000), open internal job advertising (Hirsh *et al.*, 2000), succession planning (Hirsh, 2000b), e-learning (Pollard and Hillage, 2001) and executive coaching (Carter, 2001a).

This report is not intended to be a comprehensive treatment of management development — a large and important subject. Rather, it highlights a few of the interesting questions faced by management development practitioners in assessing where we have got to in management development and where we should be heading. Our hope is that it will stimulate readers —

especially those who are practitioners themselves — to create their own visions of the future.

The structure of this report is as follows:

Chapter 2 looks at the changing context in which management development takes place, and some of the resulting challenges.

Chapter 3 provides a brief overview of some of the trends and 'new directions' in management development practice and some of the practical issues they raise. It looks at three broad forms of development: formal training and management education, informal and more personal development, and the processes for career development.

Chapter 4 summarises what the forum participants saw as their key issues in shaping the management development strategies and practices of their own organisations.

Chapter 5 looks at where we may be heading in future and some things we can be working on in the meantime.

2. The Shifting Context of Management Development

In this first chapter, we look at how the changing demands of business, and changing ideas about learning are setting challenges for management development.

2.1 Complex and turbulent organisations...

The ever-rising pressure for organisational performance stems from global competition in the private sector and the challenge to deliver better value for money in the public sector. Customers are becoming more exacting and less patient. This context is placing new demands on managers that are fundamental to the current concerns about the quality of management and leadership in the UK (CEML, 2001).

Some of the ways in which organisations seek to respond to these pressures become in themselves further challenges for managers:

- Organisations are always changing their structures and ways of working. Performance needs to be maintained at the same time as new ideas are generated. Managing effectively in perpetually turbulent organisations is the biggest challenge of all.

- Some of the organisational ideas of the 1990s place high demands on managers. Flatter structures, wider spans of control, cross-boundary working, 'virtual' teams and 'stakeholder' views of business all give managers multiple and often conflicting objectives, while reducing the amount of positional power they can use to achieve them.

- Mergers, acquisitions, and de-mergers had been a particular source of change in the organisations attending the IES forums.

Changes in ownership had led to a lot of job change and an unsettled management workforce. In one example of a de-merger, the smaller business had to become self-sufficient in managers, whereas before a large corporation had looked after the development of its managers. For several organisations, the re-alignment of corporate culture post-merger was a significant challenge for management development.

- In some organisations, faster and more flexible response is being sought by working with multiple business partners who do not share the same culture or working practices.

- Technology and e-business have been among the most visible developments of the last five years and they continue to change the nature of work and organisations.

- The IES forum participants saw issues of ethics, the environment and social responsibility as increasingly important and requiring a mature management response.

- Global businesses face an additional dimension of complexity and often of scale. They also need to find ways of working which take account of national cultures while maintaining the degree of corporate coherence they require.

2.2 ...need to find and keep good managers

These changes have a number of consequences for the types of work we have called 'management' and the types of people we have called 'managers'.

- Management is not often the first type of work that people do. Most managers are 'grown' through a series of work experiences involving increasing levels of responsibility for activities, resources, and people. Most large organisations hope to grow the majority of their managers from within the business, but also to recruit some at varied career stages. Many jobs also require a mix of managerial and professional or functional skills. Management development activity therefore needs to take account of the increasingly diverse backgrounds and career paths of managers.

- The forum participants highlighted some particular career transitions, for example that from specialist (*eg* research scientist) to manager, which present complex career and development challenges. The integration of higher level and mid-career external recruits is another big challenge in organisations that have previously grown most of their managers from within.

- The UK is generally not short on numbers of managers, but employers are concerned about their quality (Horne and Stedman Jones, 2001; Campbell et al., 2001). The IES forum participants reported shortages of good managers in some specific sectors or functions (*eg* production and manufacturing).

- Organisations all compete to recruit those mystical beings with 'high potential' or 'talent' (Chambers *et al.*, 1998). The labour markets for the best people are increasingly global. The lavish promises made in this flurry to recruit, result in some recruits, especially high quality graduates, embarking on their careers with very inflated expectations. Retention then becomes a key concern.

- Small firms and self-employment are attractive options for those with managerial skills, partly because they can respond more flexibly to the needs and interests of individuals. Large organisations can no longer assume that the best managers will want to work for them.

- Managers have gone from being the most secure of employees to being often in the front line of job cuts when organisations change ownership or structure. Organisations want their managers to be dedicated and loyal, but also to be disposable. The so-called 'psychological contract' between organisations and their managers is often fraught with tension (Herriot and Pemberton, 1995).

- Some IES forum participants were concerned that the 'burn-out' of top people is restricting both the candidate pool and the length of time people are willing to stay in critical jobs. Top public sector jobs (*eg* chief executives in the NHS) are, if anything, more exposed than executives in the private sector. Work-life balance for senior managers and executives is seen as a real, and unresolved, issue.

- In some sectors, the under-representation of women and ethnic minorities in senior positions is seen as an important issue.

2.3 Organisations want transformational leaders...

So getting and keeping the right kinds of managers is not easy. The shifting nature of organisations has also changed ideas about what a manager has to do, and the skills they need to do it. Much of this is reflected in the debate about 'leadership' and whether this is the same thing as 'management', or is a particular aspect of management, or represents a shift in ideas about management style.

Although the semantics are often sterile, the vast literature on management and leadership does highlight major challenges for managers and leaders today. Much of this literature seems to focus on the top end of management, although many of the features described apply to those with management responsibilities at any level. Managers need to ensure their organisations run efficiently, but they also need to be skilled at:

- creating a sense of vision in a fast changing environment
- motivating teams of people and leading them through change
- being innovative in products and services and ways of working.

These factors — especially of vision and motivation, but also increasingly of innovation — are often summarised in terms of moving from a 'transactional' to a 'transformational' management style (Bass, 1985). Among the attributes of transformational management listed by Bass are vision, optimism, integrity, intellectual challenge and consideration for individuals. Kets de Vries (1996) writes of the 'charismatic' versus the 'architectural' leader, and Shamir (1995) of the differences between the 'nearby' and the 'distant' leader. The word 'empowerment' is often used to signify a more motivational management style, and Argyris (1998) has linked it with the need to raise workforce commitment, especially during change.

The IES forum participants highlighted a number of skills, also seen in the research literature, needed by managers aspiring to this more transformational style:

- the ability to look ahead, to see the 'big picture' and deal with relationships (Clutterbuck and Megginson, 1999)
- teamworking, including the ability to work in teams which stretch across organisational boundaries (Colvin, 1998). This is especially challenging in complex situations, for example in mergers or business alliances (Garrow *et al.*, 2000).
- a broad understanding of business, including global issues and competitor organisations
- being able to see what technology can do to improve performance
- dealing well with change themselves, as well as being change agents for others. This is linked with self-reliance and resilience (Hiltrop, 1998) and the recently fashionable idea of 'emotional intelligence' (Goleman, 1996).

- Another way of looking at dealing with change is through continuous learning and, therefore, the meta-skill of 'learning to learn' (Winterton *et al.*, 2000) and attributes such as resilience.

So the lists of skills needed by managers grow ever longer. However, it is clear that many current concerns focus on the need to improve the personal and inter-personal skills of managers in order to lead and work with other people more effectively. Managers themselves may not always think they need inter-personal development. Mabey and Thomson (2001) found that managers placed relatively low emphasis on the need for sensitivity to others.

Although many of the skills needed by managers and leaders are common to the whole management population, they take different forms for managers at different levels and in different types of organisation. The manner in which the CEO of a major corporation leads change will be different from that of a departmental manager in the same organisation, and different yet again from the MD of a small firm.

We also need to remember that the vast majority of managers need technical and functional skills as well as more generic managerial skills.

2.4 ...who need to learn continuously

Just as there has been a shift in thinking about the nature of management and the skills needed to do it, so there have been changes in how we think about the process of learning. These changes have influenced how organisations are approaching the development of their managers.

There is wide recognition both in education and in workplace training that conveying knowledge through lectures or courses is not usually a powerful way of improving performance, especially in a field such as management where many practical skills are required.

'Competencies' have been one way of trying to articulate the desired behavioural outcomes of development. They have been used to a great extent by companies to describe management behaviour and are often used as part of performance management. Competence-based approaches to development have been particularly influential in the national approach to vocational education, increasingly defined by 'standards' and accreditation based on work-related evidence.

Interest in the fields of education and training has shifted from 'teaching' to 'learning'. The word 'learning' reminds us of the many things that may be learned and the many ways in which this learning can take place. It emphasises outcomes (what has been learned) rather than inputs (what is taught).

In this wider view of learning, more experiential and personal forms of learning have gained ground, building on the ideas of 'action learning' (Revans, 1980). Learning based on active involvement in tasks or projects is seen as a more vivid experience and more immediately relevant to the development of practical skills. Real learning may involve deep-seated changes in assumptions and attitudes as well as the acquisition of skills and knowledge. Argyris and Schon (1974) call this more challenging form of learning 'double loop learning'.

Individuals may learn best in different ways, often called 'learning styles' (from Honey and Mumford, 1982). Reflection and self-awareness is part of the learning process (Kolb, 1984). Goal setting and feedback are processes that are intended to increase such self-awareness. Technology offers new possibilities for the delivery of some learning through computers: so-called e-learning.

Learning is now seen as a continuous part of working life, and one that the individual increasingly needs to manage for themselves. Employees see access to development as an increasingly important part of their total employment package (Winter and Jackson, 1999).

Such shifts in thinking about learning have emerged gradually, but they are profound and have become a major driver for the trends in management development practice, which we examine in the next chapter.

2.5 Challenges for management development

These changes in business context, ideas about management and about how people learn, raise some real challenges for management development in employing organisations. Questions include:

Setting the Strategy

- How should organisations set and communicate their priorities for management development?

Meeting diverse needs

- In large and complex organisations, should management development be centralised or devolved?
- Can organisational management development meet the needs of the individual as well as the organisation?
- How can management development deal with an increasingly diverse management population, only some of whom stay in the organisation for a long time?

Coping with pressure

- How can development be fitted into the busy and stressful lives of managers?
- How can organisations maintain management development during their frequent experiences of organisational upheaval?

Changing delivery

- How should the methods of delivering management development take on board theories about how people learn, and the availability of ICT?
- Who should deliver management development, and what roles do HR or training professionals, line managers and employees need to play?

Evaluation

- How do we know whether management development activities are effective?

These are some of the questions we seek to address in the rest of the report as we look at key trends and issues.

3. Trends in How Managers are Developed

This chapter looks at the extent to which the changes and challenges highlighted in Chapter 2 have been reflected in management development practice. It draws mainly on published research but also on IES consultancy experience and some of the illustrations of practice shared at the IES forum events.

We will look at three main ways in which management development is delivered.

The first is the traditional main turf of management development: formal training and the running of courses, including the provision of management education in colleges and universities.

The second area we examine is the growth of what we might call personal development support, as opposed to formal training. It covers such activities as mentoring and coaching, informal workplace learning, learning sets and other facilitation of learning in small groups.

The third and final aspect of management development that we will examine in this chapter is career development. Managers, like other employees, do most of their learning through the work they do day-to-day. So the way managers move into managerial work and from one job to another is the biggest influence on what they have the chance to learn.

For each of these three aspects of management development, we examine the main trends and also some of the strategic and practical problems or issues they raise. Several of the common themes and underlying issues raised in this chapter are discussed further in Chapter 4.

3.1 Formal management training and education

3.1.1 Trends in management training

Increasing volume of management training

There was deep concern in the 1980s at the lack of training for managers in the UK, and their relatively low levels of education. Although general participation in higher education has increased sharply, there is a time lag before this shows up in the management population. Johnson and Winterton (1999) reported that 18 per cent of managers are qualified to degree level.

Thomson and Mabey have tracked the trends in corporate management development over the past fifteen years or so through large surveys of employers conducted for the Institute of Management (Thomson, Mabey *et al.*, 2001). They paint a fairly optimistic picture of management development being taken more seriously, and increases in the volume of management training taking place. Mabey and Thomson (2000) found that over the period 1996 to 2000, there had been an 18 per cent rise in formal training days for managers, and 25 per cent for those in smaller organisations. This study estimated eight days of informal training in addition to over six days of formal training per manager each year, and a training spend of £1,000 per manager per annum by those organisations able to give figures. They have found considerable emphasis within companies on junior management training, which is perhaps different from the prominence in public debate and research literature, of a concern with senior management development.

Although these studies chart the rise of informal and personal forms of development, as discussed in the Section 3.2, they do not report a downward trend in more formal training. Recent data show something of a return to formal training since the mid-1990s. Thirty-three per cent of large organisations use more informal than formal management learning, 24 per cent both equally, and 42 per cent more formal than informal (Mabey and Thomson, 2000).

This rather rosy picture of management development activity is not altogether reflected in the figures reported by individual managers through the Labour Force Survey. These show a fairly steady amount of management training activity per manager over the period 1995-2001. About 30 per cent of this training is leading to some form of qualification and this has been steady over a number of years. The LFS appears to show a shift away from off-the-job training and towards on-the-job training.

It is clear that there are still barriers to management development. Stiles *et al.* (1997) found that lack of time inhibited managers from participating in training, and also made it difficult to transfer their learning into their work.

Changing focus and methods of delivery

Within formal management training, a number of changes are evident in content and how it is delivered:

- In many organisations, management training still takes the form of key significant 'programmes' (Marx and Demby, 1998). These often signal major career transition points, *eg* first management job, entry to senior management.

- Such programmes are now less likely to be delivered in the form of a single, long, residential course, and more likely to take the form of a series of modules over a number of months with project work, and also some personal learning support in between (*eg* mentoring, coaching, learning sets).

- Although management training still covers the traditional curriculum, including finance and business strategy, change management has also been an important theme. The development of inter-personal skills — sometimes called leadership or 'soft skills' — is now seen as perhaps the most important aspect of management to learn. It is difficult, however, to improve such skills through 'chalk and talk' training; hence the greater use of other forms of learning. IES has also seen companies keen to bring business understanding and people skills together in the same programmes or events. This is especially so for senior managers who need to see their role as leaders in a holistic fashion.

- Competence frameworks have been a popular way of describing the skills needed by managers and of structuring management training (Strebler and Bevan, 1996). Major employers have tended to develop their own competence frameworks for this purpose. Holbeche (1998) gives several examples of organisations using generic leadership competencies (*eg* BP, Texaco, and Smithkline Beecham), but also warns against 'the limited shelf life of success profiles when business requirements change'.

- In some more specific aspects of management training, the trends are less clear. The 1990s saw strong interest in consortium training programmes where two or more companies design and run courses which bring their managers together (Marx and Demby, 1998). Some of the forum participants had recently reduced such involvement because it was too time consuming to set up and manage, and tended to fall apart when companies merged or re-organised. Outward bound training and team building through training was also felt by the forum participants to be of declining interest. Organisations also have different strategies with regard to in-house management colleges or training centres. Some have been sold off and others have become profit centres.

- The delivery of management training is outsourced in a variety of ways: to business schools (see below), to commercial training companies, and to very small training partnerships or freelancers. The forum participants did not see this as problematic in itself, although it does give rise to issues about how to purchase wisely in a complex market. In one case, a major international company was outsourcing management training needs analysis and design as well as delivery. This was seen as a much more complex relationship to manage.

e-Learning

There has been considerable interest in the use of computers as a means of delivering training, now called e-learning (Sloman, 2001). Some companies have used e-learning to present an electronic 'corporate university' offering a wide variety of learning modules.

Pollard and Hillage (2001) weigh up the advantages and disadvantages of e-learning. In terms of management training, the flexibility of individual access is a huge attraction, as is the ability to offer knowledge-based training more efficiently. On the downside, it may not appeal to all learners and is not easy to use for personal or 'softer' skill development. Corporate management training has also served a useful networking function within large organisations, which would be lost, if all training became electronic.

Now that the hype is beginning to die down, it seems that e-learning is going to be one of several means of delivering management training (Burgoyne, 2001). Face-to-face development of leadership skills can combine with the use of electronic communication for pre- and post-event reading, self-assessment, and follow-up email or chatroom support.

Management qualifications and the Business Schools

Business schools have become an important part of the landscape of management development (CEML, 2002). In the US, the business school MBA has moved from an elite to a mass qualification for aspiring managers. The potential impact of the more recently introduced business school DBA is as yet unclear. Some of the most best-known management gurus are business school professors, and selected schools world-wide are used as suppliers of tailored executive development to leading corporations.

In the UK, over a hundred institutions of higher education offer undergraduate or postgraduate courses in business and management. In 1999/2000, HESA recorded about 140,000 students taking higher education courses in business and management in the UK. Nearly 20,000 first degrees are awarded each year in business and management and over 11,000 higher degrees — mostly MBAs. There are around 7,000 teaching faculty in business and management studies in higher education in the UK — a very major part of the national management development resource.

An interesting feature of management higher education is that it is accessible to individuals whether or not their employers are interested in management development. They can access it before they enter employment, or study while they are working. Over 80 per cent of MBAs awarded to home students are gained by part-time study or distance learning. So there is an increasing population in the labour market who have decided for themselves to study subjects relevant to management.

Employers need to decide how to respond to the growing numbers of people who have studied management as well as how to form productive partnerships with business schools, in both management research and teaching.

3.1.2 Issues in management training

The need for corporate architecture

Organisations seem to need some clear structures and frameworks in order to provide coherent management training. The old architecture was built around big set-piece courses at various career stages — clear but rigid, and probably not wholly effective as mechanisms for learning. Competencies were the preferred architecture of the 1990s, accompanied by short, modular training events on a whole variety of specific subjects. However, the disbanding of the old courses led to a loss of coherence and resulted in a feeling of fragmentation. It may also have weakened the impact of management training on corporate culture.

IES now sees a number of employers putting core training programmes back in at key career stages, although these will now be delivered with more modern and flexible approaches. BP, for example, is just re-launching core training for its 10,000 first-line managers worldwide, which will cover both business understanding and leadership skills.

Useful development can also take place by mixing managers at different levels and career stages. One of the forum participants was moving away from a grade-based architecture for training towards mixed groups of managers from various levels of management doing their learning together.

Flexibility and rapid response

Formal management training tends to be centrally designed and delivered or purchased. This can make it slow to respond to specific training needs that arise as a result of a change in the business or a performance issue in a specific function or unit.

In addition to the main architecture for management training, some kind of 'just in time' training capability is needed. Management training budgets also need to build in this contingency.

The 'workout' approach for addressing key business issues, as used by GE and imported by other companies, combines solving business problems with an intense developmental experience.

Meeting the needs of individuals

The old-style management training courses are now often referred to pejoratively as 'sheep dips'. However, the move to shorter and modular training gives rise to issues about how individuals access the training they need, and who decides what they need. Some of the public sector forum participants felt they had gone too far in letting individuals pick courses they fancied attending, rather than those they needed. One of the international companies at the IES forums used a modular approach, but emphasised the role of the line manager in guiding the individual towards the modules they needed, within broad programmes pitched at different levels of management. This also accommodated the different past training received by individuals who had come from other companies in mid-career.

The forum participants also raised the issue of how ideas on learning styles are reflected in management training practice. In particular, a major shift to e-learning may improve training for some managers but turn off others who learn best in a more social setting.

We also need to be mindful that not all managers are accomplished and enthusiastic learners. Tamkin and Barber (1998) emphasise the need for modes of management training which help managers become more aware of their learning.

Accreditation of management training

Within the management development field, there are quite difficult issues about whether employers should link their training with some national form of quality control or accreditation.

The arguments in favour of accreditation include:

● giving employees a portable proof of the quality of management learning. For example, Arkin (2000) quotes Lloyds TSB as seeking to accredit the majority of the programmes offered through its corporate university as part of a wider HR strategy.

- The use of 'standards' and accreditation is the basis for national frameworks of vocational education. The barriers between education and workplace training are reduced if employers accredit more of the in-company training they offer.

- Accreditation may in part address the issue of measuring the outcomes of management learning (raised in the next chapter). However, it does this more at the individual level than in terms of corporate performance.

The arguments against accreditation include:

- the inflexibility and bureaucracy involved, which may focus attention away from what the business and individuals really need out of the training.

- the lack of interest in management qualifications shown by employers (Perry, 1999), especially those in small firms (Johnson and Winterton, 1999). Even managers themselves list management education leading to qualifications quite low on their preferred approaches to management development (Mabey and Thomson, 2001).

- Some employees may find accredited courses quite threatening. One of the forum participants was offering employees the choice part-way through a programme of whether to carry on to take an accredited qualification or not.

- Supporting employees in getting qualifications may lead to retention problems later on. The MBA, for example, is often used as a career passport out of the organisation. AMBA's 1997 survey found that one-third of MBA graduates leave within a year of qualifying. The forum participants were not satisfied that investment in funding MBA study had represented good value. Cost and relevance were issues here as well as retention. Some of their MBA schemes had been dropped; others were being reviewed.

Accreditation is linked in part to the idea of management as a 'profession', controlled by qualifications as other professions are. Attempts to move this way over the last ten years or so have not really worked. Williams (2000) shows that no more than seven per cent of the management population belong to relevant management associations: the IM, CIPD, marketing bodies and IoD. This may well be because the majority of managers spend their early careers in a specific field of activity and move into management later. They see management as a bundle of activities needing skills and knowledge but not as their 'profession'.

Purchasing management training

All the changes so far described mean that management development managers are often going for varied ways of delivering training (so called 'blended methods') and that much of this will be delivered by external providers. Management development managers need to become expert purchasers in an extremely complex and increasingly global market. The product they are buying needs to fit the corporate culture and the particular group of managers who will be trained. The recent CEML enquiry into management and leadership development found that employers did not feel they had enough information on the management training market to be really effective purchasers (CEML, 2002).

People skills come top of the list as the area of highest training need for managers. Yet, there are big doubts about the effectiveness of formal training interventions in producing sustained improvements in inter-personal behaviour. It is this factor which seems to have given rise to a range of other approaches to management learning based on working much more closely with individuals or small groups, as we see below.

3.2 Personal support for learning

3.2.1 Trends in personal support

The concept of tailored delivery

An IDS review of management development (1989) pointed to many of the trends we still see today. One of these trends was the strong desire to tailor training and make it useful. Usefulness to the individual learner led to arguments in favour of close collaborative personal support, such as mentoring or action learning sets, being made available to learners. This idea had been adopted by almost all of the IES forum participants over recent years.

The Anderson study of senior executives (Marx and Demby, 1998) identified individually tailored development, such as executive coaching, as likely to be more effective than standard in-company development programmes. Kettley and Strebler (1997) also reported that many companies were experimenting with more individually focussed approaches to learning including coaching, counselling and personal feedback.

More recently, the concept of tailoring training and development has centred on providing more support for learning on, or very near, the job. Coaching and project work now figure highly in the concept of 'work based' development, although Woodhall and Welchman (1998) found that 'explicit guidance on using these learning interventions is rare'.

One-to-one support for learning

A recent survey of UK management development in 500 organisations by Mabey and Thomson (2000) identified the use of mentoring and coaching as rapidly increasing. The Training and Development Survey 2001 (CIPD, 2001b) also identified the same trend, with over 80 per cent of UK companies utilising such methods to develop at least some of their people. There has certainly been a rapid increase in the use of external executive coaches (Carter, 2001a).

There are some differences of opinion about how to define and distinguish between these personal methods of supporting learning. The boundaries between what a coach, executive coach, mentor, counsellor or organisation development consultant do, are inevitably blurred. They also use similar skills. As with any relatively new type of service, some providers seem to be using labels to lay claim to the potential market.

Broadly speaking in a business context, a mentor prepares individuals to perform better in the future, and grooms them for higher and greater things, *ie* career advancement (Allen *et al.*, 1999). Some organisations have used formal mentoring schemes primarily for either graduate entrants or high potential managers, but the picture is changing. For example, one of the forum participants was mentoring ethnic minority students while they were still at university, as a means of encouraging them to join a public service organisation.

Mentors used to be drawn from the organisation's own managers (Gibbons, 2000). More recently, we have seen a trend towards hiring external mentors, especially for individuals already at a more senior level (Clutterbuck and Megginson, 1999).

Coaching is aimed at the rapid improvement of skills, behaviours and performance, usually for the current job. Coaches are trained to listen and observe, to customise for each individual's needs, and to elicit sustainable solutions and strategies from that individual. A structured and purposeful dialogue is at the heart of coaching (Lyons, 2000). The coach uses feedback and brings an objective perspective. The term 'executive coaching' basically means applying these techniques to tailoring work-related development for senior and professional managers (Carter, 2001b).

Coaching can be focused on particular events or relatively short periods of time. The NHS, for example, has offered coaching to those taking up their first post as a chief executive of an NHS Trust, to help support them through this major career transition.

Coaches have tended to be hired from outside the organisation, although IES has observed two recent changes. Firstly, the creation of internal cadres of 'professional' coaches seems to be on the increase. Secondly, the implementation of a management style called 'coaching' is gaining in popularity. In other words, some organisations (such as the Audit Commission) now expect all line managers to operate as coaches.

Whether the specific emphasis is on personal effectiveness, career aspirations or job performance, these one-to-one support processes all work in a similar way by offering personally tailored opportunities, and the mental time and space for effective reflection, and discussion of an individual's own development.

One of the reasons for the clear growth in the use of these one-to-one learning support processes seems to be their popularity with managers themselves, especially senior managers. The widespread delayering of management hierarchies of the 1990s (Kettley, 1995) has left the survivors feeling isolated and rather lonely (Herriot *et al.*, 1998). Flatter hierarchies also make the jump from one level of management to another more difficult. One-to-one support has two clear advantages for many managers. Being private, it allows the individual to discuss their development in confidence. Being personal, it can fit into a busy schedule more easily than fixed training events.

The role of feedback

Over the last ten years there has also been a rapid rise of interest in the use of personal feedback by organisations to support the individual development of its managers (Mabey and Thomson, 2001; Chivers and Darling, 1999). Usually known as multi-rater feedback or 360 degree feedback, its use quite often started with the most senior managers and then was applied to a wider management population (Kettley, 1997). The basis of such feedback is usually a framework of organisational values or competencies. These normally focus on management style and the effectiveness of managing and developing subordinates. As such, it deals more with 'soft' skills than with business skills.

360 degree feedback solicits views about a manager from the full circle of relevant viewpoints — subordinates, peers, superiors, and sometimes customers and suppliers (Tornow, 1993; London and Smithers, 1995). Self-assessment is also sometimes included. The idea is that it should provide an individual with a more accurate assessment of themselves than would be available to them from their manager or themselves alone.

The use of a feedback instrument provides a method which organisations hope will help their managers to see the skills or behaviours they need to improve. If supportive feedback is given, this can then act as a catalyst to them undertaking appropriate learning activities.

Recently we have seen an increase in the combining of personal feedback with other development methods, *eg* development centres and executive coaching. This has given more opportunities for managers to reflect on the feedback with someone who can help them interpret it in context and in a non-judgemental environment. They can also help with action planning. Without this link to action, the feedback process runs the risk of being seen as assessment rather than development.

Action learning approaches and project work

Margerison (1990) has long argued that one way to encourage managers to manage change is through action learning. Action learning sets are used to make their members consider action and promise to do it, this action usually being centred on a live work issue in their normal work environment. Managers are able to try out different approaches at work, knowing that they will have learning set colleagues who will support them in thinking through what to do and help them reflect on its impact. Horne and Stedman Jones (2001) found that project management and action learning, along with mentoring and 360 degree feedback, were felt to be the most effective forms of leadership development.

Although we have seen a steady use of action learning sets over the last ten years, it is in the related area of project working that the most recent growth appears to have occurred. Kettley and Hirsh (2000) found from their survey of managers and professionals working in cross-functional project teams that such teams are often used to expose people to different functions. Interestingly, managers in such teams had a big learning gain in personal effectiveness.

New experiences can also be gained by taking a role in another organisation. The Civil Service is using secondments as a means of achieving this. One of the forum participants mentioned encouraging non-executive directorships as another option.

Buley (1996) links the need for more challenging, or 'double-loop', learning, with the kinds of experience likely in cross-functional project teams or temporary attachments to another function or organisation. He sees such experiences as particularly helpful for younger high potential managers.

Combining personal support with formal training

Personal support approaches to development — coaching and mentoring, personal feedback and project working — are now being introduced into more traditional management development programmes. In effect, traditional off-the-job provision is reaching out to embrace aspects of on-the-job development. We also see an increase in the involvement of senior managers in the delivery of development as mentors (Alimo-Metcalf *et al.*, 2000), feedback givers and project sponsors.

3.2.2 Issues in personal support

Quality assurance and evaluation of support provision

The literature on coaching and mentoring has tended to advocate a careful matching of coach and coachee (Hall *et al.*, 1999; Carter,

2001a) or mentor and mentee (Clutterbuck, 1998) but it remains unclear how this should be done. This is an especially critical issue when the provider is going to be external and expensive. Quality is difficult to ascertain in advance and there are no widely recognised professional bodies or accreditation standards for coaches or mentors in the UK. Anyone can set themselves up in business as an executive coach.

In practice, organisations and scheme organisers have to establish their own internal mechanisms for selecting mentors and coaches. For instance, the NHS Leadership Programme has established a coaching register. Prospective coaches have to complete an application form, supply high level references and attend an interview which includes role-playing exercises. Other organisations agree guidelines or best practice operating procedures with the coaches they hire. Regular meetings between coaches and commissioners, and post-coaching interviews, also supply information about the coaches and their styles, which helps with future matching.

Personal one-to-one support approaches to management development are difficult to quality assure and evaluate because of the confidential and private nature of the process. It may be that they are inherently uncontrollable and that organisations have to accept they are to some extent taking a gamble by investing in them. They may be slightly easier to evaluate when used for a particular purpose over a limited time-frame.

Internal versus external provision

When a mentor or a coach is required to support an individual's learning, the issue arises of whether to meet that need from internal or external sources.

Internal mentors or coaches may suffer from conflicts of interest and these need to be considered in selecting a mentor or coach. For example, how can we expect individual managers to reveal something of themselves to someone who is likely to be on the assessment/selection board for their next promotion? How can a coach or mentor be expected to offer confidential support to individuals if they are asked to report talents or deficiencies to the board?

Another aspect to consider is how well the proposed coach or mentor (whether internal or external) already knows the targeted individual. It may be better for the individual to have a healthy new challenge from someone they do not already know. The learning outcomes for those individuals who have like-minded coaches and mentors are also generally regarded as less successful because a like-minded supporter will not challenge the individual's views and assumptions as much.

In general, the clear advantages of internal provision are cost and familiarity with the organisation's way of working, politics and values. The disadvantages are reduced confidentiality, lack of external view of the organisation, and the tendency to get too caught up in internal politics.

Extending to larger populations

To date, most of the personal support approaches have been mostly used for relatively small populations, mainly senior managers, high potentials and sometimes minority groups. There is an issue about the wisdom and practicality of extending the provision of personal learning support to the management population as a whole. Particular issues are:

● Some approaches are very expensive to maintain despite low initial investment costs, such as externally-provided executive coaching and the feedback-giving element of 360 degree feedback exercises.

● The success of the support is critically dependent on the quality of the individual providing the support. Organisations do not believe there is a large enough supply of really good coaches, mentors and action learning set facilitators.

● In some organisations, personal learning support is seen as 'remedial' because that is how it had been used in the past.

● There are deep concerns about our ability to evaluate these approaches although, as previously discussed, this may be easier when they are used to meet a specific need.

It seems likely that externally provided coaching and mentoring will remain of interest for a while longer and may find its place as meeting specific needs for fairly small populations. For the bulk of managers, internal provision seems a more realistic prospect.

In-house support from managers and HR specialists

There remains an issue about the skills and availability of enough internal providers to go around. This problem is exacerbated if you extend these approaches to larger populations of managers and other employees.

An emphasis on the role of the line manager as coach puts a great reliance on the willingness and ability of line managers to fulfil this role effectively. In organisations where people have traditionally been promoted into management positions on the basis of their technical knowledge, and not on their people management skills, there may be a considerable amount of development needed for many of these managers, before the concept of the manager as a coach of their own staff is realistic.

There are also issues about the availability of HR specialists to support tailored development. IES sees a rise in the number of in-house dedicated coaches, and these individuals seem to come from a variety of backgrounds, including HR. We are also seeing HR people increasingly asked by managers themselves to provide personal learning support on an informal basis. Our observation is that not all HR functions have sufficient numbers of appropriately skilled staff to respond. In particular, some management trainers may not be clear about how to balance their new role as coach with their other roles as scheme organisers, purchasers and deliverers of management development courses.

3.3 Career development

It may seem curious to some to include career development at all in a review of management development. In some organisations, the way employees move between work experiences is regarded as a matter of personnel administration. IES would argue that the sequence of jobs or work experiences which managers have is the biggest influence on how they develop.

3.3.1 Trends in career development

We have already seen in Chapter 2 that managerial careers are increasingly diverse, with more movement between organisations and less clear 'paths' to follow. How are organisations managing or supporting the careers of their managers?

Segmentation of high potential versus 'the rest'

Most large organisations still want to grow their own management to a significant extent. This leads them to want some active role in determining the kinds of career experiences that managers get. On the other hand, the possibility of managing job moves for all managers has long since gone.

The current compromise is what we might call a 'segmented' approach. This has two characteristics:

- Career development is a function of the corporate centre for what we might call 'key groups' — usually senior managers, those seen as having 'high potential' (*ie* potential for very senior or general management jobs) and sometimes corporate graduate trainees. For the majority of the managerial workforce, development is handled more locally.

- Only the 'key groups' are actively managed in terms of their careers (Holbeche, 1998; Hirsh 2000b). For example, potential general managers will often be given lateral moves between functions or business units to broaden their experiences. The majority of managers find it difficult to gain access to such moves (Hirsh, 2000a).

Succession planning linked with development

Succession planning has been around for a long time but its emphasis has gradually shifted from identifying successors for posts towards engineering the pro-active development of those successors (or 'talent pools'). The outcomes of succession planning are often developmental and focus on job experiences that would strengthen the skills and knowledge of those identified as short- or longer-term successors.

Sometimes a group of mid-career managers seen as having potential for very senior or general management posts are put on a 'high potential development programme' that may combine planned work experiences with both formal training and personal development support.

Those on such programmes can be nominated directly by senior management, but some organisations invite applicants to their high potential programmes. They then go through some kind of selection process, often an assessment centre.

Open job markets and self-managed moves

For the majority of managers, managed career moves have been replaced by open internal job markets. Internal job vacancies are increasingly advertised to employees who then apply for the next job they want. In some companies the same kind of system is being used for project opportunities as well as job moves. One of the forum participants reported that their graduate trainees now find their own job swaps between countries using the company intranet.

A study by IES (Hirsh, Pollard and Tamkin, 2000) found rapid growth in open internal job advertising. It has had a radical effect on career development. The process of internal job application in effect becomes the main process by which employees manage their careers. It amounts to a quiet revolution in personnel management with far reaching consequences.

3.3.2 Issues in career development

Weak support for career planning

Companies have been less than successful in thinking of ways to help individuals plan their own careers. In addition to open job markets as above, organisations usually advocate some form of career plan, often incorporated into a personal development plan (PDP). It is usually assumed that such planning is facilitated by a dialogue between the individual and their line manager, either in the annual appraisal or in a separate development review. Managers do not find these processes really address their career issues (Hirsh, 2000a) and the boss is often not the person they need to speak with.

Career information and advice

Managers who are taking more responsibility for their own careers need information and advice to help them make wise decisions. The provision of information and advice has been the weak link in the concept of the self-managed career. Some companies are now addressing this through the provision of career planning tools and information, often via the intranet (*eg* Lloyds TSB, Nationwide, Rolls-Royce, and Nestlé).

It is also important to be able to talk through career options with a range of other people, often informally. Recent research has shown that effective career support is much more often given informally than through formal HR processes or interventions (Hirsh, Jackson and Kidd, 2001). This raises issues about skilling managers to support employees in their career development — not just their own subordinates, but more widely. The skills for managing your own career and helping others manage theirs are not often included as part of mainstream management training.

Managers also want the HR function to be able to provide practical career support both for them as individuals and in dealing with their subordinates. This is somewhat different to the role HR has often determined for itself as a provider of systems and processes, but not actually as talking to individuals.

Managing career expectations

There is often an underlying fear in organisations that too much talk of 'careers' gives employees unrealistic expectations of promotion. Talking about careers also means talking about the future, which is uncomfortable in volatile organisations. The result has been that many managers feel no-one wants to talk about their career prospects, and the organisation would secretly like them to stay just where they are (Hirsh, 2000a). This situation leads to frustration and demotivation.

Retaining high potentials

So called 'high potential' employees create particular problems. Organisations do want them to have high expectations but this can lead to them having an inflated opinion of their abilities and a 'promote me or I'll leave' mentality. Holbeche's (1998) study of high fliers identified a number of factors that aid the retention and motivation on high performers. These included providing challenge and achievement opportunities (*eg* assignments), mentors, realistic self-assessment, and feedback processes.

The McKinsey report (Chambers *et al.*, 1998) talks in terms of the 'superior employee value propositions' required to attract and retain high potential employees. They are looking for strong values and to be well managed, to have freedom and autonomy, high job challenge and career opportunities. Retention is also dependent on good people being told they are valued.

Bevan *et al.* (1997) listed career attention and job stretch as critical factors for high potential people. Family friendly working patterns can also aid retention, but there is still a stigma in the UK in associating high potential with people who need flexible working patterns. Long hours are still *de rigeur* for those aspiring to very senior roles.

Balance of control

Although the self-managed management career has relieved the organisation of a lot of unwelcome responsibility, it causes a big shift in control. The individual determines their own career direction and the kinds of jobs they go for. The organisation of course retains the power to appoint, but has given up the power to control the direction in which someone chooses to go.

This tends to result in some jobs which are very hard to fill, for example operational as opposed to strategic roles, jobs in unglamorous locations, functions or business units. Sometimes these job roles are quite important to development as well as to the business, but individuals don't necessarily see this. Organisations need to sell the career or learning benefits of such jobs, or to adjust job design or reward package.

It does not seem feasible to put the clock back and start telling managers again that they must make a particular career move. However, a stronger steer from the organisation on which jobs to go for would often be quite welcomed by individuals.

3.4 Summary of trends

- Management development is an increasing field of activity in employing organisations.
- Management training still needs to provide a coherent view of what managers need to learn, but delivery needs to be more flexible and to fit into the busy working lives of managers.
- Organisations use external providers of management training as well as internal resources. Individuals also go to colleges and universities to access management education.

- The development of inter-personal and leadership skills is a high priority and not easily achieved through conventional formal training.

- There has been a huge growth of interest in more personal forms of development support such as coaching and mentoring.

- Most managers are now told to manage their own careers, but do so with little effective support or information.

- Line managers have been given a number of important roles in the development of their subordinates, but they may not yet be equipped to carry these out, or really be encouraged to develop others.

- High attention is often given to senior managers and 'high potential' staff, both in their skill development and in career planning. These approaches are labour intensive and not easy to extend to the majority of the management workforce.

Some of the issues raised in this chapter are reflected in the wider dialogue which the forum participants had about their own issues in management development. Their views are summarised in the next chapter.

4. Issues for Practitioners

This chapter summarises what the IES forum participants saw as their key issues. Some of them reflect the questions raised by current trends (Chapter 3) and others are broader issues about the relationship of management development to the organisation as a whole. The issues we examine cover the 'what' of management development in terms of its focus and coherence, the 'how' in terms of delivery methods, and the 'who' in terms of resourcing the activity. We end with what we might call the 'so what': issues relating to organisational learning and evaluation.

4.1 Focus and coherence in management development

What areas of learning should management development activity be focussed on and how can this be explained to employees in a coherent way?

These concerns about the focus and coherence of management development ran as a thread through the forum debates. Current approaches can feel like a lot of activity with no underpinning coherence: a course there, a learning set here, some 360 degree feedback and so on. A shift towards more personally tailored learning can also feel remote from a focus on real business issues.

4.1.1 Balancing different kinds of skill needs

Forum participants felt that different sorts of training were needed by the business and should be kept in balance. Managers need to develop functional skills and knowledge as well as generic management and leadership skills. Perhaps the generic skills have squeezed out functional training for managers over recent years. The generic skills — or 'management basics' as the participants called them — should remain a crucial part of management development. Most of the participating organisations aspired to some clear — usually modular — structure of management skill training. Organisations that had disbanded corporate management development felt that some groups of managers had missed out on basic skills and knowledge.

There also needs to be a way of responding to business-specific development needs, which can arise at short notice in a particular situation, part of the business, or management group. Examples of such specific needs included customer loyalty, post-merger integration, and e-business. What matters here is speed of response of the management development function to the business need.

4.1.2 Competence frameworks

We have already seen that many companies have defined generic and/or senior management competencies, but they vary in the extent to which these really underpin management development.

The forum participants did see a framework for describing 'basic' management skills as very important. It could provide both a means of defining management and also as a way of structuring delivery. However, the continual updating of competence frameworks was 'a chore and a distraction'. Participants felt they should aim to make such frameworks more robust and stick with them for longer. Definitions and training modules can always be adjusted within a more stable over-arching framework.

4.1.3 A central or devolved agenda

The 1980s and 1990s saw the centres of large organisations devolving much of the responsibility for management development to business streams or units. Some of the forum participants were re-centralising management development after a period of devolution and fragmentation. Even in devolved organisations, there was a desire to have a fairly corporate framework for management development. Mergers and de-mergers presented special challenges in the integration or separation of management development.

4.1.4 Looking ahead at development needs

When management development consisted largely of running courses, various processes of dialogue — largely between the management training function and senior managers — determined what courses should be run and what they should cover.

Management development is now delivered in many different ways and with individuals playing a large part in setting their own development agendas. So how do we plan for it, and how do we identify future development needs?

The forum participants touched on a number of ways of addressing the problem of planning for management development:

- Organisations need both 'top down' ways of identifying skill gaps and shifting needs and 'bottom up' ways of capturing what managers themselves see as their development needs.

- The Investors in People (IiP) approach had helped in some cases, although in others it was seen as too short-term and too much of a form-filling exercise to stimulate real debate on the quality of management.

- Business planning has often become too remote from human resource planning, so that the consequences for the management workforce and skills of expected business changes are not discussed. Top managers should be actively involved in discussing management development priorities. This also helps them to understand the relationship between management development activity and the business. Succession planning often includes a line-led overview of the resourcing and skills of the senior management population against future needs. This approach could be usefully extended to the wider management population through debate at divisional or corporate board meetings.

- At the individual level, the personal development plan (PDP) is a useful concept, but more for its thinking than as a form to be completed. PDPs can become too focussed on just the current job rather than the future, and too much constrained by competence lists and an emphasis on formal training. A more wide-ranging PDP would be more in tune with emerging ideas about development.

The participants saw dangers in spending too much time and money attempting detailed diagnoses of the individual or collective development needs of managers. Some felt it was more important to get on and do something credible, and to do it quickly. No-one claimed to have the balance spot on, but keeping some kind of balance here is important.

4.1.5 Rapid response capability

Part of this balance is about accepting the need for 'just in time' training to respond to business needs which have not been foreseen. Management development functions need to get better at budgeting for and responding to 'just in time' requests. As an aside, the term 'just in time' was seen as sounding like 'nearly too late'. Perhaps the term 'current issue' training would make the business link more apparent.

4.1.6 Improving coherence

To summarise, the forum participants saw a number of ways of increasing the sense of coherence and business relevance of management development. These approaches included:

- **competence frameworks**, but only if simple, fairly stable and continuously communicated

- **'landmarks'** at various career stages, as a useful source of both coherence and focus. These landmarks, in the form of programmes or courses pitched at the skill needs of different groups, or levels, of managers, help individuals to have a clearer framework for their changing skill needs. It is interesting to note that the term 'landmark' may be more appealing than the often-heard 'sheep dip'. Indeed, the form of such staged training may not these days be 'sheep dip' at all.

- **management development components**. Organisations should have some management development that is corporate, some local (by business stream, unit or function) and some that is individual. Clarifying the corporate components (even if these are delivered locally) helps re-establish some coherence. Focus is obtained both through corporate activities (reinforcing values and leadership) and local/individual activities (which can focus on more immediate or specific business needs).

- **collective dialogues** amongst the most senior directors and managers on management development needs.

- **integrated programmes**. Coherence can also be increased by combining different learning methods under the umbrella of integrated 'programmes'. For example, senior development programmes often include 360 feedback, personal development planning, action learning, and coaching/mentoring, as well as formal courses.

It is unlikely that management development will become coherent by going back to the rigid training structures of the past. There may be a need, however, to restrain the number of separate initiatives. Too many can lead to poor value for money, poor quality, or confused customers. For the most part, coherence is going to be about combining approaches more explicitly within some kind of corporate architecture of skills or programmes.

4.2 Balancing business with individual needs

As the delivery of management development places more control in the hands of the individual, tensions have arisen between the development that individuals choose to access and the development that the business feels they should prioritise.

Some specific concerns include:

- the difficulty of justifying very personal support, like coaching, in business terms
- the increased difficulty of forcing an individual into making a career move they don't want — often coupled with issues of mobility and lifestyle
- the experience in some organisations that the self-selection of training led to rapid reductions in training activity, or that managers sent themselves on inappropriate modules
- whether development is offered in ways which are responsive enough to individuals' varied learning styles and preferences
- lack of clarity over organisational support for employees wishing to take external qualifications.

The conclusion of this debate was that forcing individuals to develop is virtually impossible. Even if you make them go to a course, you can't make them engage their brains. However, a *laissez faire* attitude to development is equally unsatisfactory. A longer-term strategy is to try and improve the skills of all managers in managing their own learning and finding their own solutions to training needs.

This means line managers or HR professionals acting as advisers over which training modules or career moves might be most appropriate. This in turn is a matter of management culture and the extent to which responsibility for development is seen as a serious part of managing other people.

4.3 How management development is delivered

The forum participants debated a number of issues in relation to the nuts and bolts of management development practice. A few are listed below.

4.3.1 Theory and practice in learning

Although much learning theory has slipped into the vocabulary of management development (*eg* double loop learning, learning styles) there is little evidence that it is used much in practice when it comes to the design of interventions.

Some business challenges (*eg* developing entrepreneurial skills) require careful thinking about whether they can be 'taught' or are better learned in another way, or are more a matter of attitudes than of skill.

4.3.2 Social aspects of learning

The combination of one-to-one support and self-study can squeeze out the experience of learning in groups. There is a desire to keep some training collective, partly for reasons of efficiency and consistency (*eg* formal training courses) but also because the social and cultural aspects of learning are important. Small group learning (*eg* learning sets, team learning) is in some way a mid-ground between formal courses and more solitary models.

4.3.3 Accreditation of management learning

As already explored in Chapter 3, the issue of whether to try to link in-company development to external accreditation is tricky.

Although still a main plank of public policy, companies are fairly sceptical about its role in management learning. They are nervous of the need for focus and coherence (discussed in Section 4.1) being distorted by an externally imposed framework. Experience of vocational training has also led to fears of excessive time spent in form filling. The forum participants were especially concerned about the style of written work required for higher level management qualifications. One described MBAs as producing 'long dissertations of little relevance to the business'.

Some advocated working much more closely with educational institutions to try and get a more tailored approach. It remains to be seen whether the education system can meet employers halfway in providing accredited management learning that is also attractive to business.

4.3.4 Improving inter-personal skills

The current holy grail of management development is to find effective ways of improving the inter-personal skills of managers, especially those involved in the ideal of transformational leadership discussed earlier. It is one thing to appreciate the way you are supposed to behave, but quite another to sustain behavioural change.

Forum participants offered the following observations:

- 360 degree feedback plus executive coaching is a powerful lever for change.
- Facilitated action learning sets are an attractive option to support individuals in progressing personal behavioural objectives. However, they take effort to establish, and high commitment to sustain.
- For improving communication skills and confidence of individual managers, some organisations had used professional actors.
- The use of very high profile people from the outside worked well in terms of helping managers think outside the organisational box.

The old chestnut of supporting learning once people get back to their jobs was discussed. In part, learning closer to the job should reduce this gap. Encouraging desired skills and behaviour through management processes and promotion criteria was also important, especially as part of a drive to change leadership style.

4.4 The top versus the rest

A number of the types of management development described here are mostly only delivered to senior managers or younger managers seen as having 'high potential'. This list would include executive coaching, formal mentoring, business school training, succession planning and developmental job moves. Some other interventions, like 360 degree feedback and project-based development, have often started with special groups but have now spread rather more widely, albeit in slightly diluted form.

If we believe some of these approaches are effective, how might it be possible to extend some of their learning benefits to the wider management population? This probably requires significant fresh thinking, not just a 'roll out' which would be too expensive and too labour intensive.

4.5 The resourcing of management development

4.5.1 Local expertise in management development

One of the reasons for the gap between senior management development and the activity for the whole management population, is that there is often a more expert and dedicated management development resource at the corporate centre, than out in business units. Central units often have clearer responsibility for the senior population than for other managers.

Supporting management development for junior and middle managers means reaching out more effectively into the business, either through much better networking, or increased specialist presence within each business unit or function.

4.5.2 The changing role of the trainer

The forum participants preferred mainly to use external providers for management training, on the grounds that they provide a more flexible resource that you only use when needed, and that providers can be chosen with specific expertise to suit the training topic and audience. In some organisations, in-house management colleges were retained because of sector-specific needs and economies of scale. In others, there was a major in-house training resource, but used mainly for technical training (*eg* in the financial sector).

So the internal training and development function may become less involved in training delivery and more involved in a number of other activities including:

- talking to internal customers, including senior managers, about the type of development needed by the business
- finding suitable providers and managing them
- quality control and evaluation
- facilitating small group learning, including working with management teams — more of an OD and internal consulting role
- offering individual support to employees and their managers in assessing development needs and career planning.

So changing approaches to management development present some interesting challenges and opportunities to personnel and training professionals.

4.5.3 Will we all be executive coaches?

The forum participants clearly found executive coaching a hot topic. As we have seen in Chapter 3, this is an attractive form of development. The main issue raised was about whether this kind of support — at present offered only to small numbers of managers — could be used more widely.

The key barriers are those of cost and the perceived difficulty of finding enough really high quality external coaches.

Forum participants thought it likely that external executive coaches will remain as a resource mainly for very senior people, and that the use of internal coaches will increase for everyone else. Most of these internal coaches will be managers with some extra training. Some organisations are also training up their HR or training professionals as coaches.

4.5.4 The role of the line in development

Many of the issues raised in this report place new demands on managers for development of their management subordinates, their colleagues and themselves.

Coaching is but one example of such a role. We have also identified the role of the line in identifying individual and organisational development needs and in supporting career planning. Forum participants discussed how we might recognise and reward such behaviour. Recent research has shown that the best supporters of other people's development often do it for very personal reasons and because they believe it helps the business. They are little affected by exhortation from the HR function or by formal processes (Hirsh, Jackson and Kidd, 2001). Role modelling by top teams of the desired behaviour in developing others is very important in communicating that this is an important aspect of management.

4.6 The learning organisation

A number of issues related to attitudes to learning and the cultural dimension of management development.

4.6.1 From passive to active learners

Some of the public sector organisations at the forum events felt that managers were still too passive about their development and 'waited to have it done to them'. Other participants felt that wider societal change would, in time, create more demanding and self-motivated learners. There was agreement that all employees, especially managers, needed to become active learners.

4.6.2 Learning and working

The concern about finding the time for learning stems from an assumption — often at the most senior levels — that management learning is something people do in addition to their normal job. A history of taking people off on lengthy courses induced this attitude. Current approaches aim to re-integrate learning with working in a number of ways, for example through using existing projects as a means of learning rather than adding 'additional' projects to someone's workload.

4.6.3 Diversity

Diversity in management is still a major issue. Some of the recently fashionable personal interventions — like mentoring and coaching — can be seen as giving minority groups additional support. Some forum participants were concerned that such informal mechanisms may reinforce a kind of 'club' culture, and in turn delay progress towards equality of opportunity.

4.6.4 From individual development to organisational learning

The issues of organisational learning and the more fashionable phrase 'knowledge management' came up many times in discussion. The challenge is clear: how the knowledge and skills gained by individual managers can be shared with others and contribute to more effective working at organisational level. How to address this challenge is not clear at all. Early attempts to use computer technology as storehouses for learning have not really taken off. Some of the forum participants were using internal conferences and seminars to share learning. This worked better for technical knowledge than for more personal skills. Networking is clearly part of the solution: 'knowing a man [or woman] who can'. We need simpler and more effective ways of finding those who might have the knowledge or skills we need.

4.7 Evaluating management development

This report started with the business context and its impact on management development. There is increasing pressure, quite rightly, on management development managers to show that money is well spent on this activity.

Evaluation is clearly a key issue. It was a topic of high interest at the IES forums, but an area where the participants felt practice was still relatively weak.

Evaluating management development might cover:

- feedback on how well a particular intervention has worked for those involved, or of management development activity as a whole.

- the impact of management development activities on individuals' behaviour and performance.

- the impact of management development on organisational performance.

- the impact of management development on other organisational measures, *eg* employee motivation and morale.

In discussing evaluation, participants were well aware that theoretical models had been produced. They had a number of practical problems:

- Newer approaches to development, such as coaching and mentoring, are often very open-ended in their objectives and difficult to evaluate. This is partly for reasons of confidentiality, and partly because their impact may be at a deeper personal level and over longer periods of time.

- As individuals engage in varied forms of development at the same time, it is harder to untangle what of all this may be causing some change in behaviour or improvement.

- Trying to track and log all development activity goes against the notion of individual ownership, and may seem intrusive and bureaucratic.

- Proving the link between management development activity and organisational performance is hardest of all. Ironically, this is somewhat easier to see through cross-sectional studies comparing organisations, than by tracking your own organisation longitudinally. There is increasingly strong evidence that training and management development form part of the 'basket' of human resource management practices associated with superior organisational performance (Caulkin, 2001; CIPD, 2001). However, this is only the case when such development is integrated with both business strategy and individual skill needs.

The forum participants did describe the kind of evaluation methods they already use, including the examples below.

- 'Happy sheets' are still used a lot, but the desire is there to move towards measuring outcomes of learning.

- 360 degree feedback is used over time (or 'before' and 'after') to show behavioural change. There is a danger of respondent fatigue, and also concern that the samples typically used in 360 feedback may be too small to be reliable.

● Employee attitude surveys are used to monitor change at organisational level. This information is fairly easy to collect, although less detailed than 360 degree feedback, and can be tracked over longer periods of time. It has the advantage of covering both how managerial behaviour is seen by others, and how managers themselves feel about the development they receive. It still leaves cause and effect in doubt.

● Some organisations track key performance indicators (especially in the public sector) or 'balanced scorecard' organisational measures. Others are starting to conduct value chain analysis. In these methods once again, proving a link between management development activity and business improvements is very difficult.

It seems difficult for organisations to attack the issue of evaluation with any consistency. Some interventions are evaluated and others are not. Organisational indicators of performance come and go, and major re-organisations often disrupt management populations.

4.8 Summary of key issues for practitioners

In this chapter, we have reported the issues that seemed to be of greatest interest and concern to the groups of practitioners attending the IES forum events. These have included:

● the need to focus management development on organisational priorities, and to provide a sense of coherence

● reconciling the development needs of individual managers with those of the organisation

● delivering development in ways which are effective for management learning

● the challenge of extending more experiential and personal forms of development from small groups of senior managers to the whole management population

● the changing roles of trainers and of line managers in the area of management development

● influencing the learning culture of an organisation

● practical approaches to evaluating the impact of management development.

5. Future Directions?

This project set out to get a feel for where management development is at, some of the lessons to be learned from recent experiments, and whether any 'new directions' are visible.

In this final chapter we summarise what the forum participants wanted to see in the future and hazard some guesses of our own. We hope this stimulates the reader to create their own vision and areas for further work.

5.1 New millennium: new orthodoxy

Although none of the trends reported here is brand new, and some (such as action learning) have been around for many decades, what seemed to happen in the 1990s was that many of these ideas migrated from being considered somewhat 'wacky' to 'mainstream' thinking about management development.

They include recognising that:

- management has components that need to be learned
- leading people is probably the most crucial and difficult part of management
- management development has to meet the needs both of organisations and of individual managers
- experiential and personal forms of learning are often more vivid than classroom teaching
- constructive feedback, especially on specific behaviours, is a lever for raising self-awareness and facilitating change.

5.2 What practitioners want to see

Our inability to predict the future was seen to be a central problem in management development. However, that did not prevent the IES forum participants from sharing their thoughts about what a positive future for management development might contain:

- training and development leading the business not following it; maintaining investment in 'bad times'

- continued emphasis on 'learning to learn', active self-managed learning and the desire to tailor training to individual need. Likely continuation in the use of 360 degree feedback.

- getting the individual to do more of the work in organising their own learning and careers, supported by open information on (a) what the company requires in terms of values, functional skills, business awareness and (b) what career and learning opportunities are available

- basic management training in place with a process to ensure that individuals do receive the training they need; using internal provision where quantity of demand is significant and high quality can be provided

- additional learning, targeted at specific short-term business needs, and delivered quickly

- continued emphasis on both informal and facilitated group learning; finding new ways for people to share their learning both electronically and by meeting others

- more emphasis on evaluation and organisational learning

- increasing use of e-learning, although not necessarily seen as dominating or substituting for other forms of learning

- new ways of working with educational institutions to deliver relevant and challenging business education

- a greater role for professional bodies/networks in individuals' learning; companies need to understand what support these varied bodies are offering their employees

- a strong external focus through networking (at individual and organisational levels) and non-executive directorships, secondments *etc.*

- stronger pools of internal mentors and coaches, and the encouragement of individuals to take more responsibility for finding someone to support them (perhaps from some kind of internal database)

- more transparent succession planning systems and a reduction in ageism in identifying and developing 'high potential' (with more women included in such groups)
- HR taking a lead with the development of its own people.

5.3 What further changes seem likely?

As recent trends work their way through, what are we likely to see?

- individuals who are more demanding about development and more accustomed to managing their own learning
- a more global debate about effective management — perhaps less dominated by the US
- a global market for those who can provide the best learning experiences for executives, with some close partnerships between companies and Business Schools
- a growing expectation by individuals and senior managers that management development managers must be expert purchasers of management development services
- more networks and associations of external suppliers, *eg* of executive coaches (Parsloe, 2001), Business Schools
- e-learning taking its place and becoming more genuinely interactive — person to person via machine, not just person to machine
- better educated managers, including more coming through who have already studied business or management at university, and/or take part-time postgraduate courses
- integration of management training into initial and continuing professional training in a wide range of professions
- more research on management learning, including its effectiveness and business impact.

5.4 A more integrated approach

There are some tensions apparent in management development thinking which raise some interesting choices and uncertainties about future direction.

One tension is around the focus for development. Companies wish to focus on investment in learning that will make a difference to productivity. Individuals have their own learning agendas driven by interest, the desire for personal growth, career goals and the need to remain employable. Will companies continue to widen their management development agendas to include much of the agendas of their employees, partly as a means of attracting and retaining talent, but also because leadership is a very personal matter? Or will the need to show a clear link between the management development agenda and the business, cause a re-focusing on a narrower and more specific set of business skills and knowledge areas?

Another tension concerns how development will be delivered. The models of learning currently advocated by learning theory are holistic, experiential, learner-driven, and exploratory: rather close in fact to a well-facilitated playgroup sandpit. The pressure to show measurable results can move us towards narrow learning objectives and ways of measuring: rather like recent trends in secondary schools with the national curriculum, SATs, and league tables. e-Learning looks likely to accelerate the provision of management learning in highly controlled 'bite sized' chunks, with the possibility of recording an assessment at the end of each chunk. Will the pressure to show measured results drive out more innovative and experiential approaches to management learning?

A third tension is about who investment goes into. The language of training and development often makes the assumption that everyone can get better at everything given a chance: long lists of competencies, lots of feedback, training courses on how to be entrepreneurial. Most people — including psychologists — believe that aptitudes, attitudes and early socialisation restrict how much we can really change as adults. So when resources are limited, do we invest in the most talented managers (because they can have the biggest impact on the business), or the poor performers (who might get better), or the bulk of managers in the middle (because they are all being asked to do more)?

These three tensions above might easily lead to a growing gap between the 'luxury' provision of tailored and personally supported development for the most senior managers, and a more cheaply delivered, more standardised form of management development (possibly more via e-learning) for the majority of managers. Will market forces lead to the development of high

Figure 5.1: Management development — a more integrated approach

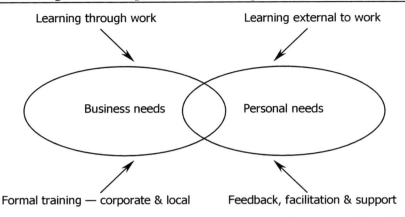

Learning through work

Learning external to work

Business needs

Personal needs

Formal training — corporate & local

Feedback, facilitation & support

Source: IES

quality *and* affordable development provision for the majority of managers, or will it be second rate and 'dumbed down'?

Of course, it is artificial to see these tensions as leading to mutually exclusive choices. Figure 5.1 shows the possibility of a more integrated model of management learning — a kind of 'horses for courses' approach. Multiple methods of development seem likely to persist — the new jargon term being 'blended methods'. These will also come from multiple sources of provision, and may meet different needs.

Individual managers will find some of their development needs being met by their employers through formal training, but should also expect to invest in their own learning outside work through education, professional bodies and personal networks.

The rather expensive models for facilitated support, which we have seen develop as formal mentoring and coaching, seem likely to become more informal as they spread to larger populations of managers. This links with the huge potential for 'learning through work'. Organisations could be very much better at designing development into normal managerial jobs, organisation structures and career moves, as well as encouraging on-the-job coaching.

Institute for Employment Studies

5.5 Things to be working on

However we think these tensions will be played out — and fashions will surely come and go — there seem to be some aspects of management development which organisations need to address more energetically in the short term:

- better quality line-led reviews of overall strengths and weaknesses in the management population

- more appropriate blending of different modes of delivery: training events, personal support and e-learning

- better information on career options and training opportunities easily available to all employees

- better dialogue with individuals about their learning needs and preferences, and career direction

- training for all employees on how to manage their own careers and development

- stronger emphasis within core management training on 'developing others'

- some HR people with more specialised skills in giving career advice and coaching

- faster response to specific business issues ('just in time') and local training needs

- more stable corporate architecture for management learning with continuous adjustment replacing tendency to launch-scrap-relaunch

- reducing the learning provision gap between 'the top' and 'the rest' of the management population

- clearer communication of the management development offer and processes

- more practical approaches to organisational learning

- more sustained and practical efforts at evaluation.

Bibliography

Allen T D, McManus S E, Russell J E A (1999), 'Newcomer Socialization and Stress: Formal Peer Relationships as a Source of Support', Journal of Vocational Behavior, Vol. 54, pp. 453-470

Alimo-Metcalf M, Ford J, Harding N, Lawler J (2000), *Leadership Development in British Organisations*, Careers Research Forum

AMBA (1997), *MBA Salary and Career Survey*, Association of MBAs

Argyris C, Schon D A (1974), *Theory in Practice: Increasing Professional Effectiveness*, Jossey-Bass

Argyris C (1998), 'Empowerment: The Emperor's New Clothes', *Harvard Business Review*, May-June

Arkin A (2000), 'Combined Honours', *People Management*, 12 October

Bass B M (1985), *Leadership and Performance Beyond Expectations*, London: Free Press

Bevan S, Barber L, Robinson D (1997), *Keeping the Best: a practical guide to retaining key employees*, IES Report 337

Bosworth D (1999), *Empirical Evidence of Management Skills in the UK*, Skills Task Force Research Paper 18, DfEE

Buley T (1996), *Aiming for the Top*, Careers Research Forum

Burgoyne J (2001), *Corporate E-learning*, Careers Research Forum

Campbell M, et al. (2001), *Skills in England 2001: Key messages*, DfES

Carter A (2001a), *Executive Coaching: Inspiring performance at Work*, IES Report 379

Carter A (2001b), 'The trainer as executive coach', *Training Journal*, Ely: Fenman, December

Caulkin S (2001), 'HR and the bottom line: the time is now', *People Management*, 30 August, pp. 32-34

Institute for Employment Studies

CEML (2001), *Meeting the Need: a Consultation Paper*, London: Council for Excellence in Management and Leadership

CEML (2002), *The Contribution of the UK Business Schools to Developing Managers and Leaders*, London: Council for Excellence in Management and Leadership

Chambers E, Foulon M, *et al.* (1998), 'The War for Talent', *McKinsey Quarterly*

Chivers W, Darling P (1999), *360-Degree Feedback and Organisation Culture*, London: Institute of Personnel and Development

CIPD (2001a), *The Change Agenda: People Management and Business Performance*, London: CIPD

CIPD (2001b), *Training and Development, 2001 Survey Report*, London: CIPD

Clutterbuck D (1998), *Learning Alliances: Tapping into Talent*, London: IPD

Clutterbuck D, Megginson D (1999), *Mentoring Executives and Directors*, Oxford: Butterworth-Heinemann

Colvin G (1998), 'Revenge of the nerds', *Fortune*, Vol. 137, No. 4, 2 March, pp. 223-224

Dale M, Bell J (1999), *Informal Learning in the Workplace*, Research Brief RB134, DfEE, August

DfEE (2000), *Skills for all: Proposals for a National Skills Agenda*, final report of the National Skills Task Force, DfEE

Doyle M (1995), 'Organisational Transformation and Renewal: A Case for Reframing Management Development', *Personnel Review*, Vol. 24, No. 6

DTI (2000), *The Future of Corporate Learning*, DTI

DTI (2001), *UK Competitiveness Indicators*, 2nd Edition, DTI

Ford R (1991), 'Developing Winners: The Importance of Executive Coaching', *Human Relations*, Issue 2, pp. 113-116

Gaertner K, Nollen S (1989), 'Weak Link and Strong Links: Employee Commitment and Performance', in Niehaus R, Price K (eds), *Human Resource Strategies for Organizations in Transition*, Plenum Press

Garrow V, Devine M, Hirsh W, Holbeche L (2000), *Strategic Alliances − Getting the People Bit Right*, Roffey Park Institute

Gibbons A (2000), 'Getting the most from mentoring: recent developments and learning', *Training Journal*, Ely: Fenman, March

Goleman D (1996), *Emotional Intelligence*, London: Bloomsbury

Hall D T, Otazo K L, Hollenbeck G P (1999), 'Behind Closed Doors: What Really Happens in Executive Coaching?', *Organisational Dynamics*, Winter

Herriot P, Pemberton C (1995), *New Deals*, Chichester: John Wiley & Sons

Herriot P, Hirsh W, Reilly P (1998), *Trust and Transition: Managing Today's Employment Relationship*, Chichester: John Wiley & Sons

Hiltrop J M (1998), 'Preparing people for the future', *Strategic Change*, Vol. 7, No. 4, June-July, pp. 213-221

Hirsh W (2000a), *Career Development for the Core Management Workforce*, Careers Research Forum

Hirsh W (2000b), *Succession Planning Demystified*, IES Report 372

Hirsh W, Pollard E, Tamkin P (2000), *Free, Fair and Efficient? Open Internal Job Advertising*, IES Report 371

Hirsh W, Jackson C, Kidd J M (2001), *Straight Talking: Effective Career Discussions at Work*, Cambridge: CRAC/NICEC

Holbeche L (1998), *High Flyers and Succession Planning in Changing Organisations*, Roffey Park Institute

Holbeche L (1999), *Aligning Human Resources and Business Strategy*, Oxford: Butterworth Heinemann

Honey P, Mumford A (1982), *The Manual of Learning Styles*, Maidenhead: Peter Honey

Hopfl H, Dawes F (1995), 'A Whole Can of Worms — The Contested Frontiers of Management Development and Learning', *Personnel Review*, Vol. 24, No. 6, pp. 19-28

Horne M, Stedman Jones D (2001), *Leadership: the challenge for all?* Institute of Management

Huselid M (1995), 'The impact of human resource management practices on turnover, productivity and corporate financial performance', *Academy of Management Journal*, Vol. 38(3), pp. 635-72

IDS Top Pay Unit (1989), *Management Development*, Research File

Johnson S, Winterton J (1999), *Management Skills*, Skills Task Force Research Paper 3, September, DfEE

Kets de Vries M (1996), 'Leaders Who Make a Difference', *European Management Journal*, Vol. 14, No. 5

Kettley P (1995), *Employee Morale During Downsizing*, IES Report 291

Kettley P (1997), *Personal Feedback: Cases in Point*, IES Report 326

Kettley P, Hirsh W (2000), *Learning from Cross-functional Teamwork*, IES Report 356

Kettley P, Strebler M (1997), *Changing Roles for Senior Managers*, IES Report 327

Klasen N, Clutterbuck D (2002), *Implementing Mentoring Schemes*, Oxford: Butterworth-Heinemann

Kolb D A (1984), *Experimental Learning*, Englewood Cliffs NJ: Prentice Hall

Labour Force Survey, National Statistics

London M, Smithers J W (1995), 'Can multi-source feedback change perceptions of goal accomplishment, self-evaluations, and performance related outcomes? Theory based applications and directions for research', *Personnel Psychology*, Vol. 48

Lyons L S (2000), 'Coaching at the heart of strategy', in Goldsmith M, Lyons L, Freas A, *Coaching for Leadership*. San Francisco: Jossey-Bass/Pfeiffer

Mabey C, Thomson A (2000), *Achieving Management Excellence*, Institute of Management

Mabey C, Thomson A (2001), *The Learning Manager*, Institute of Management

Margerison C (1990), 'The Way Managers make their Organisations Succeed', *Leadership and Organisation Development Journal*, Vol. 11, No. 4, pp. 17-22

Marx E, Demby N (1998), *Grooming for the Board — How the top 200 UK Companies Select, Develop and Remunerate their Senior Managers*, London: Arthur Anderson

Nevins M, Stumpf S (1999), '21st century leadership: redefining management education', *Strategy and Business*, Vol. 3, Issue 16

Parsloe E (2001), 'Searching for standards: defining a professional framework', *Training Journal*, Ely: Fenman, December

Patterson M, West M, Lawtorn R, Nickell S (1997), *Impact of People Management Practices on Business Performance*, Issues in People Management, No. 22, Institute of Personnel and Development

Perry B (1999), *The Influence of Qualifications on Career Progress*, Careers Research Forum

Pollard E, Hillage J (2001), *Exploring e-Learning*, IES Report 376

Revans R (1980), *Action Learning: New Techniques for Management*, London: Blond and Briggs

Sangster C (2000), 'Squaring the circle: 360 degree mentoring', *Training Journal*, Ely: Fenman, November

Shamir B (1995), 'Social Distance and Charisma', *Leadership Quarterly*, Vol. 6, pp. 19-47

Sloman M (2001), *The e-Learning Revolution*, London: CIPD

Stiles P, Gratton L, Truss C, Hope-Hailey V, McGovern P (1997), 'Performance management and the psychological contract', *Human Resource Management Journal*, 7(1), pp. 57-66

Strebler M, Bevan S (1996), *Competence-based Management Training*, IES Report 302

Tamkin P, Barber L (1998), *Learning to Manage*, IES Report 345

Thomson A, Mabey C, Storey J, Gray C, Iles P (2001), *Changing Patterns of Management Development*, Oxford: Blackwell

Thomson A, Storey J, Mabey C, Gray C, Farmer E, Thomson R (1997), *A Portrait of Management Development*, London: Institute of Management

Thomson A, Storey J, Mabey C, Thomson R, Gray C, Farmer E (1998), *Management Development, The views of the membership of the Association of MBAs*, Association of MBAs

Tornow W W (1993), 'Perceptions or reality: Is multi-perspective measurement a means or an end?' *Human Resource Management*, Vol. 32, pp. 221-230

Williams S (2000), *Management and Leadership Teaching: Present Trends and Future Demand*, CEML

Winter J, Jackson C (1999), *Riding the Wave*, Career Innovation Research Group

Winterton J, Parker M, Dodd M, McCracken M, Henderson I (2000), *Future Skills Needs of Managers*, DfEE Research Report RR182

Woodhall J, Welchman R (1998), *Work-based Management Development*, Kingston Business School for the IPD

Institute for Employment Studies